Foundational Skills

Phonics
for First Grade

cherries

hen

SHELL EDUCATION

Contributing Authors

Jodene Smith, M.S.

Mary Rosenberg, M.A.Ed.

Suzanne I. Barchers, Ed.D.

Chandra Prough, M.A.Ed.

Christine Dugan, M.A.Ed.

Publishing Credits

Robin Erickson, *Production Director;* Lee Aucoin, *Creative Director;* Timothy J. Bradley, *Illustration Manager;* Sara Johnson, M.S.Ed., *Editorial Director;* Evelyn Garcia, *Editor;* Grace Alba, *Designer;* Corinne Burton, M.A.Ed., *Publisher*

Standards

© 2010 National Governors Association Center for Best Practices and Council of Chief State School Officers (CCSS)

Shell Education

5301 Oceanus Drive
Huntington Beach, CA 92649-1030
http://www.shelleducation.com
ISBN 978-1-4258-1098-6
© 2014 Shell Education Publishing, Inc.

Table of Contents

Developing Foundational Skills in Reading

Foundational Skills: Phonics for First Grade has been written with first graders in mind! The pages in this book provide children practice with some of the foundational skills needed to be successful readers—phonics and word recognition.

There has been much written and said about phonics. All the talk has left questions about what phonics is and whether it should be taught. Simply put, phonics is the relationship between letters and sounds. When a child learns that the letter *s* makes the /s/ sound, that is phonics! Since children need to be able to figure out words in order to read, it is important that they understand the relationship between the letters that are on the page and the sounds the letters make (Chall 1995).

There has been much research to show that phonics needs to be explicitly taught and included in good reading programs. In fact, the National Reading Panel (2000) included phonics as one of the five essential components of reading instruction. The fact is that a large number of words in English do follow patterns and rules. Instruction and practice with phonics gives children an opportunity to develop their understanding of the relationship between letters and sounds. Additionally, researchers have found that phonic awareness is a strong predictor of later reading achievement (Juel 1988; Griffith and Olson 1992; Lomax and McGee 1987; Tunmer and Nesdale 1985).

But not all words can be figured out with phonics (Cook 2004). For example, the words *of* and *the* cannot be sounded out with knowledge of letter and sound relationships. There are several word lists that have been compiled of words that occur in print with high frequency, and many of these words do not follow patterns and rules (Fry and Kress 2006). Children need to know other ways to read or figure out words that they cannot apply phonics to, such as recognizing words by sight or using context. For this reason, practice with frequently occurring grade-level-appropriate sight words is an important component of reading.

This book provides children with many opportunities to practice key skills in both phonics and word recognition. Practicing these skills helps build the foundation for successful readers. And although the traditional saying is "practice makes perfect," a better saying for this book is "practice makes successful readers."

Understanding the Standards

The Common Core State Standards were developed through the Common Core State Standards Initiative. The standards have been adopted by many states in an effort to create a clear and consistent framework and to prepare students for higher education and the workforce. The standards were developed as educators worked together to incorporate the most effective models from around the country and globe, to provide teachers and parents with a shared understanding of what students are expected to learn at each grade level, and as a continuum throughout the grades. Whereas previously used state-developed standards showed much diversity in what was covered at each grade level, the consistency of the Common Core State Standards provides educators a common understanding of what should be covered at each grade level and to what depth.

The Common Core State Standards have the following qualities:

- They are aligned with college and work expectations.

- They are clear, understandable, and consistent.

- They include rigorous content and application of knowledge through high-order skills.

- They build upon strengths and lessons of current state standards.

- They are informed by other top-performing countries so that all students are prepared to succeed in our global economy and society.

- They are evidence based.

Students who meet these standards within their K–12 educations should have the skills and knowledge necessary to succeed in their educational careers and beyond.

Name: _____ **Date:** _____

Directions: Write the letters *-ap* to finish each word. Then read the words. Draw a line from each word to its picture.

1. l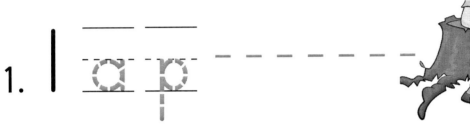

2. c

3. m

4. n

5. t

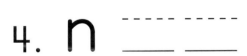

One-Syllable Words

Name: _____ **Date:** _____

Directions: Write the letters *-at* to finish each word. Then read the words. Draw a line from each word to its picture.

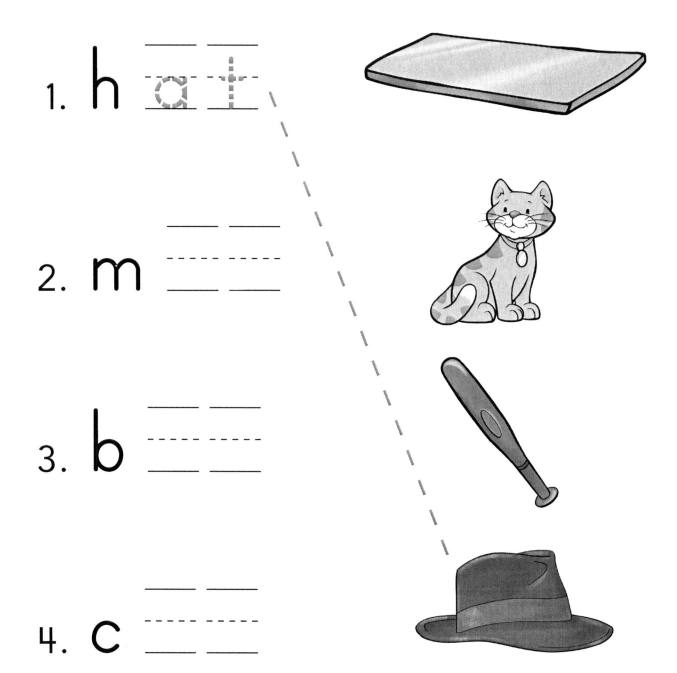

1. h a t

2. m _ _ _

3. b _ _ _

4. c _ _ _

One-Syllable Words

Name: _____ **Date:** _____

Directions: Write the letters *-ig* to finish each word. Then read the words. Draw a line from each word to its picture.

1. j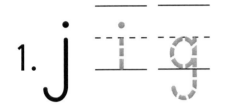

2. b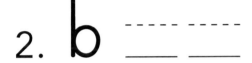

3. d

4. w

5. p

One-Syllable Words

Name: _____ **Date:** _____

Directions: Write the letters *-in* to finish each word. Then read the words. Draw a line from each word to its picture.

1. d

TOWEL

2. w ___ ___ ___

3. b ___ ___ ___

4. p ___ ___ ___

5. f ___ ___ ___

Name: _____ **Date:** _____

Directions: Write the letters *-ip* to finish each word. Then read the words. Draw a line from each word to its picture.

1. t i p

2. h ___ ___

3. r ___ ___

4. s ___ ___

5. d ___ ___

One-Syllable Words

Name: _____ **Date:** _____

Directions: Write the letters *-it* to finish or complete each word. Then read the words. Draw a line from each word to its picture.

1. p 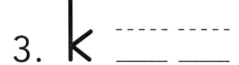 i t

2. h _____

3. k _____

4. m _____ t

5. b _____

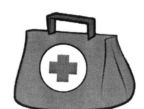

Name: _____ **Date:** _____

Directions: Write the letters *-ot* to finish each word. Then read the words. Draw a line from each word to its picture.

1. t o t

2. p ___ ___ ___

3. d ___ ___ ___

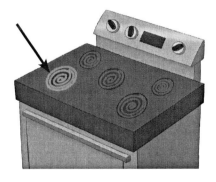

4. h ___ ___ ___

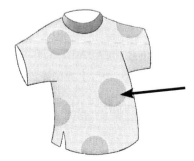

One-Syllable Words

Name: _____**Date:** _____

Directions: Write the letters *-en* to finish each word. Then read the words. Draw a line from each word to its picture.

1. B

2. p _____

3. h _____

4. m _____

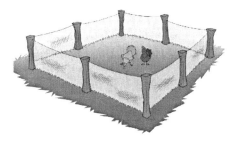

5. t _____

Name: _____ **Date:** _____

Directions: Write the letters *-et* to finish each word. Then read the words. Draw a line from each word to its picture.

1. m

2. j _ _ _

3. p _ _ _

4. n _ _ _

5. v _ _ _

One-Syllable Words

Name: _____ **Date:** _____

Directions: Write the letters -*ug* to finish each word. Then read the words. Draw a line from each word to its picture.

1. b u g

2. j ____ ____

3. r ____ ____

4. m ____ ____

5. h ____ ____

Name: _____ **Date:** _____

Directions: Write the letters -*ut* to finish or complete each word. Then read the words. Draw a line from each word to its picture.

1. c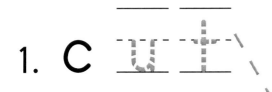

2. n ___ ___

3. m ___ ___ t

4. h ___ ___

Long Vowel *a*

Name: _____ **Date:** _____

Directions: Say the name of each picture. The letters are mixed up. Spell the word correctly in the blank.

1. 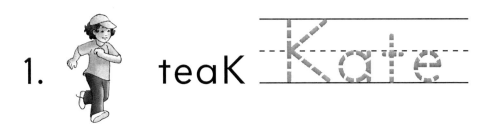 teaK ‾K‾a‾t‾e‾

2. kace _____

3. 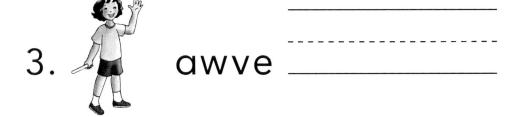 awve _____

4. krae _____

5. dsate _____

Name: _____ **Date:** _____

Directions: Read the words in the box. Choose the correct word to complete each sentence. Write the word in the blank.

Jake	~~rake~~	cake	lake	take

1. Kate can _rake_.

2. Kate bakes a _____.

3. Kate races to the _____.

4. Kate will _____ dates.

5. Kate waves to _____.

Long Vowel e

Directions: Read each sentence. Circle the correct word to complete each sentence. Write it in the blank.

1. I like to eat __<u>meat</u>__.

    (meat) meet

2. I want to _____ Pete.

    meat   meet

3. I was home for a _____.

    weak week

4. Pete likes to eat _____.

    leaks leeks

5. I like to swim in the _____.

    see sea

Name: _____ **Date:** _____

Directions: Read the sentences. Circle the correct word to complete each sentence. Write it in the blank.

1. The giant is _____.

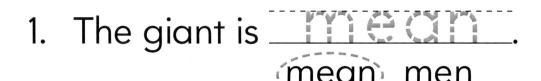

(mean)   men

2. I will _____ a king.

meet   met

3. Pete _____ a book.

reads   red

4. The queen took a _____.

seat   set

5. The hen _____ her chicks.

fed   feeds

Long Vowel *i*

Name: _____ Date: _____

Directions: Read each sentence. Underline the words with the long *i* sound.

1. Mike can spy the pile.

2. Can you spy the bike and trike?

3. Mike likes fries and pie.

4. I see a fly in the sky.

5. The dime is by the lime.

Long Vowel *i*

Name: _____ **Date:** _____

Directions: Read the sentences. Finish each sentence with the word that rhymes. Write it in the blank.

1. I am Mike. I like to __hike__ .
   high dive (hike)

2. He can fly. He flies _____ .
   nine high up

3. It is night. I lit the _____ .
   mind light sky

4. What can you find? Make up
   your _____ .
   glide mind time

Long Vowel *i*

Directions: Say the name of each picture at the beginning of the row. Read the words. Think about the vowel sound in each word. Circle the words that have the same vowel sound as the picture.

1.    kit    Mike    smile

2.   spy   fix   mind

3. 9   high   crime   in

4.   fire   his   fix

5.    my   fight   it

Name: _____ **Date:** _____

Directions: Read the words in the box. Choose the correct word to complete each sentence. Write the word in the blank.

| Rose | broke | slope | ~~store~~ |

1. Mom went to the ___store___.

2. Dad fixed a lace that _____.

3. Dad pulled Rose in a _____.

4. _____ rode down a slope.

Long Vowel *o*

Directions: Read each sentence. Circle the correct word to complete each sentence. Write it in the blank.

1. Bose does not like his __coat__.

   cote ~~coat~~

2. Rose likes to _____ Bose.

   comb come

3. Bose does not like _____.

   sope soap

4. Rose plays with her _____.

   boat bote

5. Bose likes his _____.

   boan bone

Long Vowel *o*

Name: _____ **Date:** _____

Directions: Say the name of each picture. The letters are mixed up. Spell the word correctly in the blank.

1.  owcr

2.  stoens _____

3.  oatfl _____

4.  daot _____

5.  noce _____

Long Vowel *u*

Name: _____ Date: _____

Directions: Read the sentences. Underline the words with the long *u* sound.

1. <u>Luce</u> and <u>Bruce</u> are friends.

2. Drew likes to run on the dunes with Bose.

3. Rose has a cute blue hat.

4. Sue packs up fruit cubes.

5. Luce sings a tune.

Name: _____ **Date:** _____

Directions: Read the sentences. Circle the correct word to complete each sentence. Write the word in the blank.

1. The hat is __cute__.

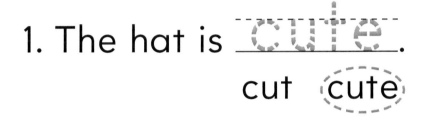

cut (cute)

2. Luce said, "Hi, _____!"

dud   Dude

3. Luce cut up _____ of fruit.

cubs   cubes

4. A _____ is made of sand.

dun   dune

5. Luce likes to swim with a _____.

tub   tube

Short Vowel Practice

Name: _____ **Date:** _____

Directions: Change the vowel in each word to name the picture. Write the new word in the blank.

1.		rug _____
2.		mop _____
3.		pan _____
4.		hut _____
5.		dog _____
6.		nut _____

Name: _____ **Date:** _____

Directions: Circle the word that names the picture.

1. (jam) jim jum	2. tab tob tub
3. lag leg lug	4. dad did dod
5. wag wig wog	6. fax fix fox

Short Vowel Practice

Name: _____ **Date:** _____

Directions: Answer each question. Circle *yes* or *no.*

1. 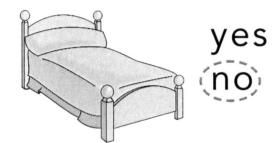 yes (no) Can a bed dig?	2. yes no Is a bag tan?
3.  yes no Is a pig pink?	4.  yes no Can a cat skip?
5.  yes no Can a mop win?	6.  yes no Can a hen peck?

Short Vowel Practice

Name: _____ **Date:** _____

Directions: Circle the correct word.

1. It lives in a pen. (pig) peg	
2. It goes on your head. cup cap	
3. You have two of them. leg lag	
4. It can lick you. dig dog	
5. A dad gives it. hag hug	
6. You eat it. nut net	

Long Vowel Practice

Name: _____ **Date:** _____

Directions: Fill in the blanks with vowels to spell the words. Rewrite the word.

1. c a k e c a k e	2. n _ n _ _ _ _ _
3. b _ k _ _ _ _ _	4. n _ t _ _ _ _ _
5. h _ s _ _ _ _ _	6. t p _ _ _ _ _

Long Vowel Practice

Name: _____ **Date:** _____

Directions: Add an *e* to the end of each word to make it a long vowel word.

1. 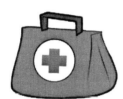 _____
   ## pin

2.  _____
   ## can

3.  _____
   ## kit
   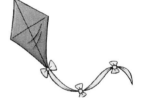

4.  _____
   ## tub

5.  _____
   ## cap

6.  _____
   ## cub

Long Vowel Practice

Name: _____ **Date:** _____

Directions: Circle the missing word.

1.  It is going to _____. ran (rain)	2.  He will go on the _____. boat bot
3. We will plant a _____. seed sed	4. 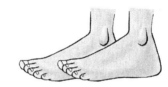 She will wash her _____. fet feet
5.  We made a _____. lin line	6.  The dog wags his _____. tail tal

Long Vowel Practice

Name: _____ Date: _____

Directions: Write the words to name the pictures. Circle the vowel team in each word.

Word Bank
snow   pie   ~~hay~~   tie   pay   blow

1. _h(ay)_	2. _____
3. _____	4. _____
5. _____	6. _____

Syllables

Name: _____ **Date:** _____

Directions: Write the one-syllable nouns. Circle the vowel in each word.

Word Bank

hat   fish   pen   ~~milk~~   dress   desk

1. m i l k

2.

3.

4.

5.

6.

Syllables

Name: _____ **Date:** _____

Directions: Look at the animal names. Divide each word into syllable parts.

1. camel

ca/mel

2. zebra

3. kitten

4. rabbit

5. parrot

6. hamster

Syllables

Name: _____ Date: _____

Directions: Circle the number of syllables in each word.

1.  sock   1   2   3

2.  wagon   1   2   3

3.  lamp   1   2   3

4.  triangle   1   2   3

5.  spider   1   2   3

6.  bell   1   2   3

Syllables

Name: _____ **Date:** _____

Directions: Write the number of syllables.

1.	**2.**
3.	**4.**
5.	**6.**

Syllables

Name: _____ **Date:** _____

Directions: Write the number of syllables.

1. _____ - - - - - - - - - - _____	2. _____ - - - - - - - - - - _____
3. _____ - - - - - - - - - - _____	4. _____ - - - - - - - - - - _____
5. _____ - - - - - - - - - - _____	6. _____ - - - - - - - - - - _____

Syllables

Name: _____ **Date:** _____

Directions: Write each word. Count the number of syllables.

```
┌─────────────────────────────────────────────────────┐
│                     Word Bank                        │
│   duck    window    pencil    music    umbrella    s̶t̶a̶m̶p̶s̶   │
└─────────────────────────────────────────────────────┘
```

1.   stamps   1

2.   _____   _____

3.   _____   _____

4.   _____   _____

5.   _____   _____

6.   _____   _____

Syllables

Name: _____ **Date:** _____

Directions: Count the syllables. Write the words in the correct column.

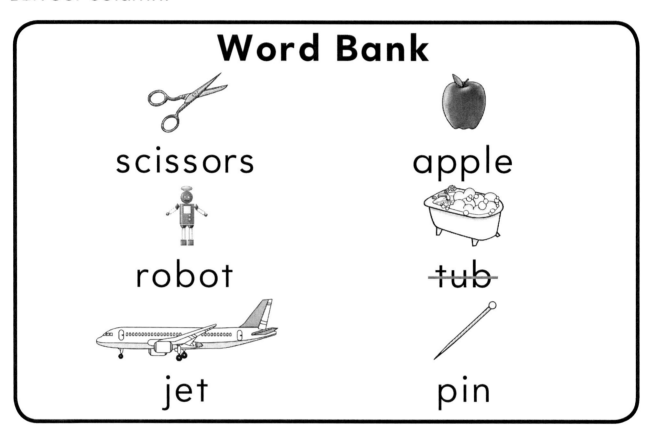

Word Bank

scissors   apple

robot   ~~tub~~

jet   pin

1 Syllable	2 Syllables
tub	

Name: _____ **Date:** _____

Directions: Circle the number of syllables in each compound word.

1.  baseball 1 ② 3	2.  hotdog 1 2 3
3.  backpack 1 2 3	4.  grasshopper 1 2 3
5.  sunflower 1 2 3	6.  basketball 1 2 3

Two-Syllable Words

Name: _____ **Date:** _____

Directions: Draw a line between the double consonants to divide each word into two syllables.

1. carrot	2. bunny
3. apple	4. mattress
5. arrow	6. button

Two-Syllable Words

Name: _____ **Date:** _____

Directions: Draw a syllable line between the double consonants. Circle the word that names the picture.

1. balloon bottle

2. ribbon rabbit

3. penny puppy

4. ladder lettuce

5. butter bubble

6. summer soccer

Compound Words

Name: _____ **Date:** _____

Directions: Combine the words to make a compound word.

1.	star	+ fish	= *starfish*
2.	cup	+ cake	= _____
3.	cow	+ boy	= _____
4.	lip	+ stick	= _____
5.	pony	+ tail	= _____
6.	lady	+ bug	= _____

Name: _____ **Date:** _____

Directions: Draw a syllable line between the consonants in the words in the Word Bank. Then, write the word for each clue.

Word Bank

pen/cil   window

helmet   elbow

1. you write with this

   ___pencil___

2. you wear this when you bike

   _____

3. where your arm bends

   _____

4. you look out this

   _____

Two-Syllable Words

Name: _____ **Date:** _____

Directions: Match the words to the pictures. Then, draw a syllable line between the two consonants to separate the word into the two syllable parts.

1. `sister`

2. _____

3. ⬤ _____

4. _____

5.  _____

6. **15** _____

Name: _____ **Date:** _____

Directions: Match the words to the pictures. Then, draw a syllable line after the first vowel to separate the word into the two syllable parts.

1. o/val

2. paper

3. bacon

4. tiger

5. zero

6. baby

0

Two-Syllable Words

Name: _____ **Date:** _____

Directions: Match the words to the pictures. Then, draw a syllable line to separate the word into syllable parts.

Word Bank

salty	~~farmer~~	windy
friendly	fearful	tallest

1.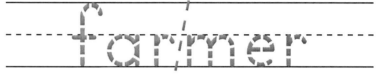

2.

3.

4.

5.

6.

Two-Syllable Words

Name: _____ **Date:** _____

Directions: Write how many syllables each picture has. Then, complete the crossword puzzle.

Word Bank

forest   butter   gopher

wagon   ~~rainbow~~

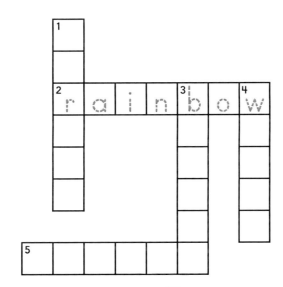

Across:

2. _2_____

5. _____

Down:

1. _____

3.  _____

4. _____

Inflectional Endings

Name: _____ **Date:** _____

Directions: Underline the base in each word. Circle the ending.

1.  rides

2.  eats

3.  walks

4.  reads

5.  sits

6.  blows

Name: _____ **Date:** _____

Directions: Underline the base in each word. Circle the ending.

1.  <u>wait</u>(ing)

2.  thinking

3.  playing

4.  helping

5.  climbing

Inflectional Endings

Name: _____ **Date:** _____

Directions: Underline the base in each word. Circle the ending.

1.  <u>fill</u>(ed)

2.  painted

3.  kicked

4.  spilled

5.  stretched

6.  yelled

Name: _____ **Date:** _____

Directions: Underline the base in each word. Circle the ending.

1.  <u>draw</u>(s)

2. 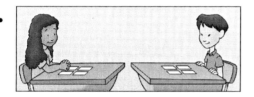 studying

3.  teaching

4.  whispered

5.  traces

6.  watered

Inflectional Endings

Name: _____ **Date:** _____

Directions: Write each word below using the *-s*, *-ing*, and *-ed* endings. Practice reading the words.

	-s	-ing	-ed
jump	jumps	jumping	jumped
stomp			
add			

Name: _____ **Date:** _____

Directions: Read each sentence. Circle the correct word to complete each sentence.

1. Mike _____ to school yesterday.

   walks   walking   (walked)

2. She _____ to slide.

   likes   liking   liked

3. Max is _____ at the book.

   looks   looking   looked

4. The man _____ on the house.

   works   working   worked

5. We are _____ grandma.

   visits   visiting   visited

Irregularly Spelled Words

Name: _____ **Date:** _____

Directions: Read the sentence. Fill in the bubble with the correct word.

1. I am going _____ a party.	⬤ to ◯ tu
2. I _____ not want to miss it.	◯ du ◯ do
3. Sam _____ six years old.	◯ wuz ◯ was
4. I _____ a gift for him.	◯ have ◯ haav
5. _____ had cake for us.	◯ Thay ◯ They

Irregularly Spelled Words

Name: _____ **Date:** _____

Directions: Read each word. Circle the picture and word that rhymes with the word.

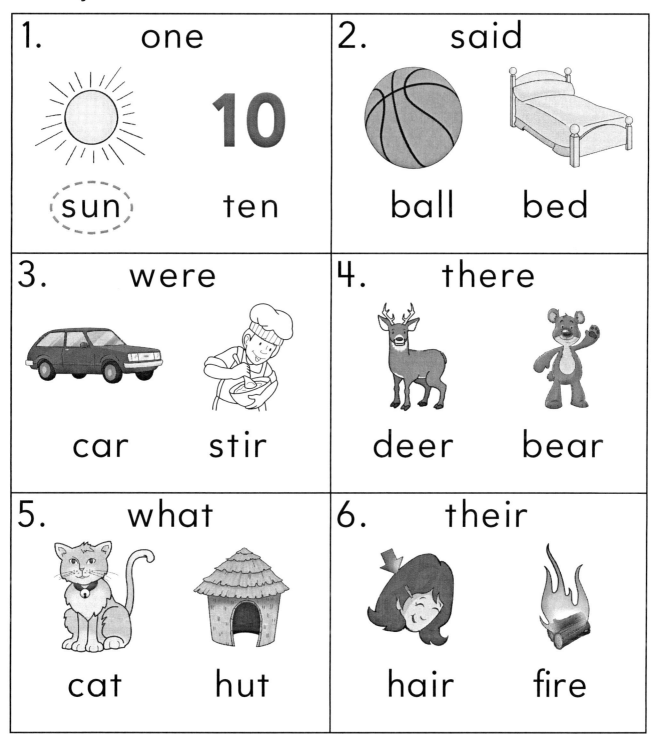

1. one
   10
   sun   ten

2. said
   ball   bed

3. were
   car   stir

4. there
   deer   bear

5. what
   cat   hut

6. their
   hair   fire

Irregularly Spelled Words

Name: _____ **Date:** _____

Directions: Complete the crossword puzzle by using words from the word bank. Write the words in the blank.

Word Bank
about   some   would
~~people~~   two   could

Across:
1. Look at all the ___people___.
2. The story was _____ a bear.
3. The dog _____ catch a ball.

Down:
4. I ate _____ apples.
5. She _____ like to come along.
6. She wants _____, too.

Irregularly Spelled Words

Name: _____ **Date:** _____

Directions: Read each sentence. Fill in the bubble for the sentence that matches the picture.

1. know		⬤ I know how to yell. ◯ I know that girl.
2. come		◯ We will come to your house. ◯ He can come to school.
3. for		◯ The apple is for Tom. ◯ Mom has a cake for you.
4. who		◯ Who can run fast? ◯ Who is at the door?
5. been		◯ He has been sick. ◯ We have been at the park.
6. find		◯ The dog will find the bone. ◯ She cannot find her pencil.

Irregularly Spelled Words

Name: _____ **Date:** _____

Directions: Unscramble the word to complete the sentence. Use the Word Bank.

Word Bank

does	Put	~~from~~
any	once	only

1. mrof	The gift is _____from_____ my mom.
2. yna	Do you have _____ milk?
3. cone	Run around the track _____.
4. lyon	She _____ has an apple for lunch.
5. tPu	_____ your jacket on.
6. sdoe	He _____ his work well.

Irregularly Spelled Words

Name: _____ **Date:** _____

Directions: Count the items. Write the number word.

Word Bank
three   one   two   four   six   five

1. _____ four	2. _____
3. _____	4. _____
5. _____	6. _____

Irregularly Spelled Words

Name: _____ **Date:** _____

Directions: Draw lines to match the pictures and words.

1.    woman

2.    boy

3.    baby

4.    man

5.    people

6.    girl

Irregularly Spelled Words

Name: _____ **Date:** _____

Directions: Draw lines to match the sentences and pictures.

1. I *know* you are by the tree.

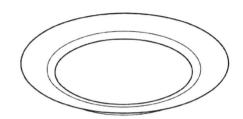

2. There are *no* cookies left.

3. She can *write* with a pencil.

4. He got the *right* book.

$$2 + 2 = 4$$

5. The *sum* of 2 and 2 is 4.

6. Mom wants *some* more hugs.

References Cited

Chall, Jeanne S. 1995. *Learning to read: The great debate*, 3rd ed. Orlando: Harcourt Brace.

Cook, Vivian. 2004. *Accomodating brocolli in the cemetary: Or, why can't anybody spell?* New York: Touchstone.

Fry, Edward B., and Jacqueline E. Kress. 2006. *The reading teacher's book of lists*, 5th ed. San Francisco: Jossey-Bass.

Griffith, Priscilla L., and Mary W. Olson. 1992. Phonemic awareness helps beginning readers break the code. *The Reading Teacher*, 45: 516–523.

Juel, C. 1988. Learning to read and write: A longitudinal study of 54 children from first to fourth grades. *Journal of Educational Psychology*, 78: 243–255.

Lomax, Richels G., and Lomax M. McGee. 1987. Young children's concepts about print and meaning: Toward a model of reading acquisition. *Reading Research Quarterly*, 22: 237–256.

National Governors Association Center for Best Practices and Council of Chief State School Officers. 2010. Common core standards. http://corestandards.org/the-standards.

National Reading Panel. 2000. *Report of the National Reading Panel: Teaching children to read*. Washington, DC: Donald N. Langenberg, chair.

Tunmer, William E., and Richard A. Nesdale. 1985. Phonemic segmentation skill and beginning reading. *Journal of Educational Psychology*, 77: 417–427.

Answer Key

page 11

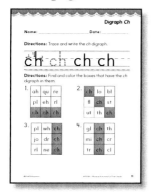

page 15

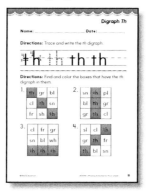

page 19

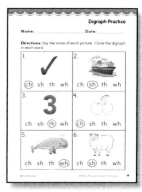

page 12

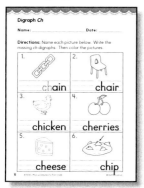

page 16

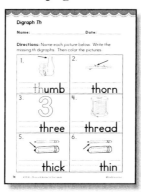

page 20

page 13

page 17

page 21

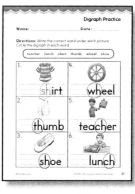

page 14

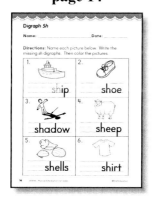

page 18

page 22

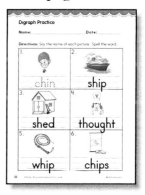

Answer Key *(cont.)*

page 23

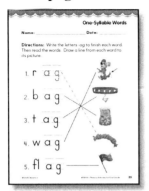

page 27

page 31

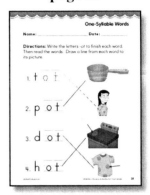

page 24

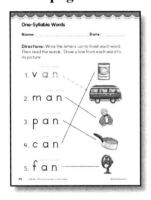

page 28

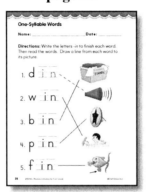

page 32

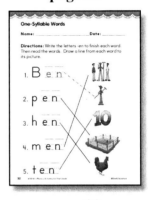

page 25

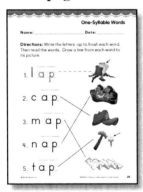

page 29

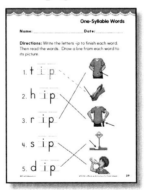

page 33

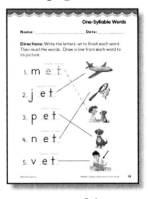

page 26

page 30

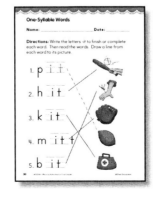

page 34

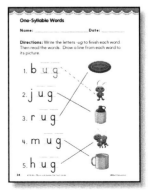

page 35

One-Syllable Words

Name: _____ Date: _____

Directions: Write the letters -ut to finish or complete each word. Then read the words. Draw a line from each word to its picture.

1. c u t
2. n u t
3. m u t t
4. h u t

page 36

Long Vowel *a*

Name: _____ Date: _____

Directions: Say the name of each picture. The letters are mixed up. Spell the word correctly in the blank.

1. teaK — Kate
2. kace — cake
3. awve — wave
4. krae — rake
5. dsate — dates

page 37

Long Vowel *a*

Name: _____ Date: _____

Directions: Read the words in the box. Choose the correct word to complete each sentence. Write the word in the blank.

Jake ~~rake~~ cake lake take

1. Kate can rake.
2. Kate bakes a cake.
3. Kate races to the lake.
4. Kate will take dates.
5. Kate waves to Jake.

page 38

Long Vowel *e*

Name: _____ Date: _____

Directions: Read each sentence. Circle the correct word to complete each sentence. Write it in the blank.

1. I like to eat meat. (meat) meet
2. I want to meet Pete. meat (meet)
3. I was home for a week. weak (week)
4. Pete likes to eat leeks. leaks (leeks)
5. I like to swim in the sea. see (sea)

page 39

Long Vowel *e*

Name: _____ Date: _____

Directions: Read the sentences. Circle the correct word to complete each sentence. Write it in the blank.

1. The giant is mean. (mean) men
2. I will meet a king. (meet) met
3. Pete reads a book. (reads) red
4. The queen took a seat. (seat) set
5. The hen feeds her chicks. fed (feeds)

page 40

Long Vowel *i*

Name: _____ Date: _____

Directions: Read each sentence. Underline the words with the long *i* sound.

1. Mike can spy the pile.
2. Can you spy the bike and trike?
3. Mike likes fries and pie.
4. I see a fly in the sky.
5. The dime is by the lime.

page 41

Long Vowel *i*

Name: _____ Date: _____

Directions: Read the sentences. Finish each sentence with the word that rhymes. Write it in the blank.

1. I am Mike. I like to hike. high dive (hike)
2. He can fly. He flies high. nine (high) up
3. It is night. I lit the light. mind (light) sky
4. What can you find? Make up your mind. glide (mind) time

page 42

Long Vowel *i*

Name: _____ Date: _____

Directions: Say the name of each picture at the beginning of the row. Read the words. Think about the vowel sound in each word. Circle the words that have the same vowel sound as the picture.

1. kit (Mike) (smile)
2. (spy) fix (mind)
3. (high) (crime) in
4. (fire) his fix
5. (my) (fight) it

page 43

Long Vowel *o*

Name: _____ Date: _____

Directions: Read the words in the box. Choose the correct word to complete each sentence. Write the word in the blank.

Rose broke slope ~~store~~

1. Mom went to the store.
2. Dad fixed a lace that broke.
3. Dad pulled Rose in a slope.
4. Rose rode down a slope.

page 44

Long Vowel *o*

Name: _____ Date: _____

Directions: Read each sentence. Circle the correct word to complete each sentence. Write it in the blank.

1. Bose does not like his coat. cote (coat)
2. Rose likes to comb Bose. (comb) come
3. Bose does not like soap. sope (soap)
4. Rose plays with her boat. (boat) bote
5. Bose likes his bone. boan (bone)

page 45

Long Vowel *o*

Name: _____ Date: _____

Directions: Say the name of each picture. The letters are mixed up. Spell the word correctly in the blank.

1. owcr — crow
2. stoens — stones
3. oatfl — float
4. daot — toad
5. noce — cone

page 46

Long Vowel *u*

Name: _____ Date: _____

Directions: Read the sentences. Underline the words with the long *u* sound.

1. Luce and Bruce are friends.
2. Drew likes to run on the dunes with Bose.
3. Rose has a cute blue hat.
4. Sue packs up fruit cubes.
5. Luce sings a tune.

Answer Key *(cont.)*

page 47

Long Vowel *u*

Name: _____ Date: _____

Directions: Read the sentences. Circle the correct word to complete each sentence. Write the word in the blank.

1. The hat is **cute**.
   cut (cute)

2. Luce said, "Hi, **Dude**!"
   dud (Dude)

3. Luce cut up **cubes** of fruit.
   cubs (cubes)

4. A **dune** is made of sand.
   dun (dune)

5. Luce likes to swim with a **tube**.
   tub (tube)

page 51

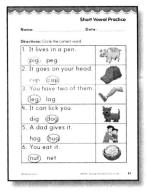

Short Vowel Practice

Name: _____ Date: _____

Directions: Circle the correct word.

1. It lives in a pen.
   (pig) peg

2. It goes on your head.
   cup (cap)

3. You have two of them.
   (leg) lag

4. It can lick you.
   dig (dog)

5. A dad gives it.
   hag (hug)

6. You eat it.
   (nut) net

page 55

Long Vowel Practice

Name: _____ Date: _____

Directions: Write the words to name the pictures. Circle the vowel team in each word.

Word Bank
snow pie hay tie pay blow

1. **hay**
2. **pay**
3. **tie**
4. **pie**
5. **snow**
6. **blow**

page 48

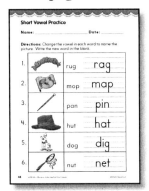

Short Vowel Practice

Name: _____ Date: _____

Directions: Change the vowel in each word to name the picture. Write the new word in the blank.

1. rug → **rag**
2. mop → **map**
3. pan → **pin**
4. hut → **hat**
5. dog → **dig**
6. nut → **net**

page 52

Long Vowel Practice

Name: _____ Date: _____

Directions: Fill in the blanks with vowels to spell the words. Rewrite the word.

1. cake **cake**
2. nine **nine**
3. bike **bike**
4. note **note**
5. hose **hose**
6. tape **tape**

page 56

Syllables

Name: _____ Date: _____

Directions: Write the one-syllable nouns. Circle the vowel in each word.

Word Bank
hat fish pen milk dress desk

1. **milk**
2. **desk**
3. **pen**
4. **dress**
5. **fish**
6. **hat**

page 49

Short Vowel Practice

Name: _____ Date: _____

Directions: Circle the word that names the picture.

1. (jam) jim jum
2. tab tob (tub)
3. lag (leg) lug
4. (dad) did dod
5. wag (wig) wog
6. fax fix (fox)

page 53

Long Vowel Practice

Name: _____ Date: _____

Directions: Add an e to the end of each word to make it a long vowel word.

1. **pine**
2. **cane**
3. **kite**
4. **tube**
5. **cape**
6. **cube**

page 57

Syllables

Name: _____ Date: _____

Directions: Look at the animal names. Divide each word into syllable parts.

1. camel **ca/mel**
2. zebra **ze/bra**
3. kitten **kit/ten**
4. rabbit **rab/bit**
5. parrot **par/rot**
6. hamster **ham/ster**

page 50

Short Vowel Practice

Name: _____ Date: _____

Directions: Answer each question. Circle yes or no.

1. Can a bed dig? yes (no)
2. Is a bag tan? (yes) no
3. Is a pig pink? (yes) no
4. Can a cat skip? yes (no)
5. Can a mop win? yes (no)
6. Can a hen peck? (yes) no

page 54

Long Vowel Practice

Name: _____ Date: _____

Directions: Circle the missing word.

1. It is going to _____ ran (rain)
2. He will go on the _____ (boat) bot
3. We will plant a _____ (seed) sed
4. She will wash her _____ fet (feet)
5. We made a _____ lin (line)
6. The dog wags his _____ (tail) tal

page 58

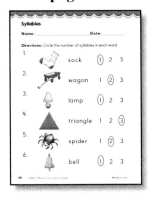

Syllables

Name: _____ Date: _____

Directions: Circle the number of syllables in each word.

1. sock (1) 2 3
2. wagon 1 (2) 3
3. lamp (1) 2 3
4. triangle 1 2 (3)
5. spider 1 (2) 3
6. bell (1) 2 3

page 59

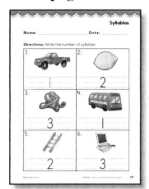

page 63

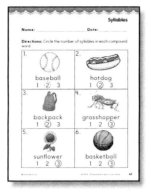

page 67

page 60

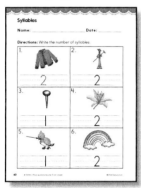

page 64

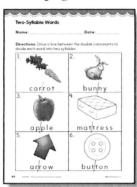

page 68

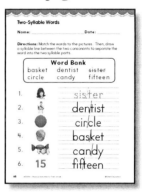

page 61

page 65

page 69

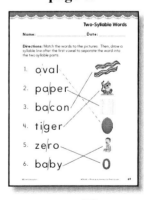

page 62

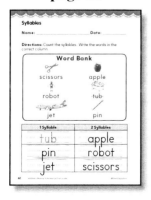

page 66

page 70

Answer Key *(cont.)*

page 71

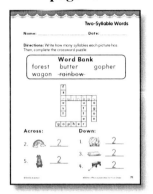

page 75

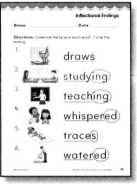

page 79

page 72

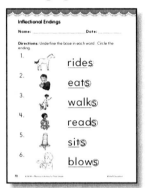

page 76

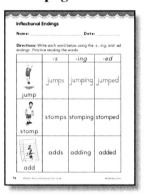

page 80

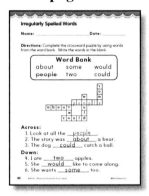

page 73

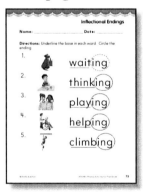

page 77

page 81

page 74

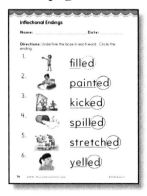

page 78

page 82

page 83

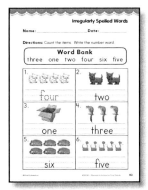

page 84

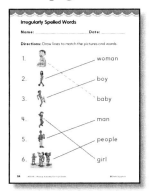

page 85

Contents of the Digital Resource CD

Page	Filename
11	page11.pdf
12	page12.pdf
13	page13.pdf
14	page14.pdf
15	page15.pdf
16	page16.pdf
17	page17.pdf
18	page18.pdf
19	page19.pdf
20	page20.pdf
21	page21.pdf
22	page22.pdf
23	page23.pdf
24	page24.pdf
25	page25.pdf
26	page26.pdf
27	page27.pdf
28	page28.pdf
29	page29.pdf
30	page30.pdf
31	page31.pdf
32	page32.pdf
33	page33.pdf
34	page34.pdf
35	page35.pdf
36	page36.pdf
37	page37.pdf
38	page38.pdf
39	page39.pdf
40	page40.pdf
41	page41.pdf
42	page42.pdf
43	page43.pdf
44	page44.pdf
45	page45.pdf
46	page46.pdf
47	page47.pdf
48	page48.pdf
49	page49.pdf

Page	Filename
50	page50.pdf
51	page51.pdf
52	page52.pdf
53	page53.pdf
54	page54.pdf
55	page55.pdf
56	page56.pdf
57	page57.pdf
58	page58.pdf
59	page59.pdf
60	page60.pdf
61	page61.pdf
62	page62.pdf
63	page63.pdf
64	page64.pdf
65	page65.pdf
66	page66.pdf
67	page67.pdf
68	page68.pdf
69	page69.pdf
70	page70.pdf
71	page71.pdf
72	page72.pdf
73	page73.pdf
74	page74.pdf
75	page75.pdf
76	page76.pdf
77	page77.pdf
78	page78.pdf
79	page79.pdf
80	page80.pdf
81	page81.pdf
82	page82.pdf
83	page83.pdf
84	page84.pdf
85	page85.pdf

Notes

Notes